Parents Who Don't Do Dishes

(and other recipes for life)

RICHARD MELNICK

Contents

Dec 1, 2012

For Mary –

With Best Wishes –

Richard Melnick

Days up and down they come
Like rain on a conga drum
Forget most, remember some
But don't turn none away

To live is to fly
Both low and high
So shake the dust off of your wings
The sleep out of your eyes

~Townes Van Zant
"To Live Is To Fly"

Author's Note

I was not quite 24-years-old, sitting in my best friend Marko's apartment in New York City, when in walked a beautiful blue-eyed woman of about 18 years. I instantly recognized her as someone who would be important to me, though she didn't give me a second look. Eventually, we became friends and would go to the occasional movie, hang out, talk—just pals. That is until many years later, on the evening of Marko's funeral, when Alice and I became something more.

We were buddies for six years, dated for three, married for twelve, divorced, and have been friends again for the past eleven years. Whew! We've been co-parenting for nearly 18 years and I feel extraordinarily fortunate to have had such a thoughtful friend for the past three decades. Without Alice, my most precious life experiences—knowing our boys, Jackson and Josh—would never have happened. She has the steel of a lawyer, the soul of a poet, and is an avid practitioner of kindness and quick wit. She willingly fills in the blanks of my memory (including a few things I'd prefer to forget), and I will always feel gratitude and affection for her. Accordingly, this book is dedicated to her, without whom I might be doing my own dishes.

And a special tip of the hat to the town of Crested Butte, an extraordinary community that has nurtured and supported, challenged and exhilarated our boys. Thanks from the bottom of my heart. This is for you, too.

Disclaimers

I sometimes write in a declarative style though I don't presume to know what's true or best for everyone. Play with the ideas. Accept or reject them in whole or in part.

Our life isn't entirely the fairy tale that's portrayed as we still enjoy the occasional meltdown and shit-storm.

Everyone must be willing to grow…at the end of the day, no parent can teach their child how to be kind, authentic, create boundaries and manage reactivity without doing those same things themselves. But when kids and adults are growing together, magic *is* possible.

And I still help with dishes now and then.

Foreword

As a cancer patient with three- and five-year-old boys, I knew first hand of the fears of the day: Who would father my sons? Would they miss me? Would they forget about me? How would Alice and the kids manage financially? The permutations of painful outcomes were beyond my grasp.

I gained peace by asking myself over and over, "What am I afraid of right now, in this moment?" And the answer was always the same: nothing. My fears were all based on the future.

I was alive now.

And for that matter, when I investigated the pain I felt in the moment, it became humorous how much my belly hurt from the chemotherapy. When I demanded to know if I would live, I'd smile kindly and remind myself that this also was a concern set in the future.

I *was* alive—right now.

I reminded myself that in the present moment, perhaps the most easily expressed emotion is gratitude. For this breath. And the next. And the next. Maybe gratitude is an essential ingredient for healing.

Why waste life being stuck in our heads, avoiding pain, avoiding life, when instead we can dive deeply into both pleasure and pain with equanimity and intensity? This seems the masterful approach. Stop seeing everything as good and bad, right and wrong. *"To live is to fly, both low and high, so shake the dust off of your wings, the sleep out of your eyes,"* wrote Townes Van Zant.

Fears of an untimely death must have informed my parenting style as I felt a sense of urgency to pass along life lessons. I also stayed focused on celebrating "who they are now," as opposed to feeling a need to change them in any way. And I wanted them to participate deeply in the truth of their life as an operating philosophy. To quote the psychologist Bruce Tift, I wanted them to "be willing to feel, aware of their feelings and aware of awareness." I also wanted them to have a strong work ethic to ensure their survival.

Through it all, I still had a sense of the possibility of seeing Jackson (who was entering first grade) graduate from high school and watching Josh begin to grow into a man too. And now, twelve years later, I appreciate you taking the time to bear witness to my journey as I reflect on the consequences of my parenting style, intended and otherwise.

The title of this book came during a heated conversation with my friend Robin Cox, the mother of twin 10-year-old boys. We were discussing how to encourage service around the house, manage reactivity, respect individual sovereignty, provide effective consequences, offer compassion and empathy without needing to fix anything, and how to use precise and conscious language. At some point, to get her attention I exclaimed, "I'm going to write a book called *Parents Who Don't Do Dishes!*"

Eventually, Robin had an epiphany—that by setting good boundaries for herself, letting life flow without yelling and cajoling, without her need to have things just so, she witnessed what she called, "the beauty of the death of control."

Hopefully some of these perspectives, and a few of our favorite recipes, will find a place in your heart (and stomach) too. Food is one of my loves, and teaching my boys to cook at an early age seemed important. I've also included a mystical component which may provide a rationale to dive deeply into the practice of immediacy, aliveness . . . and that sink of dishes!

Introduction

Wouldn't it be a pleasure to have the dishwasher loaded and unloaded like clockwork, the pots and pans washed, the kitchen swept, counters cleaned and food properly put away without even thinking about it? This scenario plays an active role in my fantasy life, up there with dating Sophia Vergara and heli-skiing Bella Coola.

My boys Josh and Jackson are now 15- and 17-years-old, and though we share equally in the cooking, cleaning the kitchen remains their domain. And given our small town lifestyle, it's easy for them to do other stuff like shopping and random errands too. Occasionally, I actually feel as though I'm living in a five star hotel, my kids the cheerful concierge. Did someone say foot massage?

Although, to be sure, I taught them by serving them, including squeezing their little (and eventually big) feet with love. Well aware of my unconditional devotion, they've also discovered that I'm not their butler, cook, nor majordomo.

In addition to practical skills like cooking and cleaning, they've also learned other life lessons and discovered that unlike a sink of dirty dishes, there's often no tidy resolution to many situations. Accordingly, they're able to skillfully handle anything life throws at them and the accompanying range of emotions.

They've learned that expecting life to be free from outside disturbance and internal conflict is a fantasy.

They've learned to not play the victim and, for the most part, to participate in life as it is in the moment—whether it's happy, sad, anxious, or whatever.

They've become comfortable with the unknown and they've learned to develop a playful relationship with disturbance.

And above all else, my boys have learned the inherent benefit of practicing kindness no matter what—kindness toward self and kindness toward others. So when I ask them to clean the kitchen before they go out, even if their internal response is, "That's bullshit!" they transform it into, "No problem, Dad. It'll only take a few minutes."

They've discovered the paradox that as we do for others we do for ourselves. And they've learned that by keeping healthy boundaries they take responsibility for their lives and accordingly are able to offer *true* compassion, free from neediness or neurotic codependency.

Then again, their response to my request to clean the kitchen may not transform into action, giving *me* the opportunity to keep good boundaries and offer my own compassion: "Wow. You think I'm a terrible dad? That must be painful for you! Let me give you a hug."

Feelings and Basic Stuff

I remember one peaceful day, sitting on the rocks above Grant Lake in the late summer afternoon near our home in Crested Butte, grateful to be alive. The boys were about three- and five-years-old and we didn't have any agenda. I just began rambling out of the blue...

"Feeling the truth of your being at any given moment is the doorway to experiencing deep aliveness...I believe you have a soul that doesn't die when your body is gone, and essentially, death is an illusion."

I told them that we could send love to their Grandpa Phil who had recently died and that he could feel it right now. It rang true for them and they seemed comforted and excited. Sitting on the rocks, surrounded by wild sage and overlooking the lake, we practiced sending love to Grandpa Phil and the look on their faces was one of pure rapture.

I suggested that the same energy that created their souls also infused their body and all other forms of matter. Every blade of grass, every bug, bird, animal, every rock, every mountain, the stars in the sky, and of course every person are all created from the same Basic Stuff. Everything and everyone deserves respect and love because everywhere you look, if you're aware, you see yourself. You remember your Greater Nature.

By having these conversations at a very early age maybe they understood the words like music, remembering the melody from deep within without needing to recite the notes and chord changes. Maybe this gave them a helpful counterpoint to the process of individuation that childhood entails—reminding them of their Greater Nature. They seemed to develop a deep reverence for life and an underlying sense of ease as they moved through the world. They were not the kind of kids to squish a bug or anything else, and from an early age I consistently heard reports about how unusually kind they were.

(*For another religious experience, try* **Brian's Potato Salad**. *It's THE bomb, the first recipe in the book for good reason.*)

That same afternoon sitting on the rocks overlooking the lake I told my little darlings "Take off your mask and be authentic." By authenticity, I also meant giving your passion and talent and integrity to the world. I believe this is your sacred duty. Maybe your creative force is expressed as a farmer or a doctor or musician or maybe it's standing on your head or rubbing your dog's tummy. It's all good. The creative force knows no limit of expression.

I also told my boys that if they paid close attention, they could differentiate between thinking and feeling. You can hear a voice in your head that is distinct from the feelings you have and some people refer to this voice as the ego. The ego is always finding something wrong with what's happening now, or as Jimmie Dale Gilmore sings, *"My mind has a mind of its own."* The mind often wants to tell a story about the past or future, label the present good or bad or somehow resist the moment, wrestle you away from experiencing the truth and bliss of your Greater Nature.

I suggested that unlike thinking, feelings are a full-body sensation and not inherently harmful. Feelings come and go if they are not resisted. I asked them to notice how the voice in their head is different than the feeling they have when they hug a puppy, cry uncontrollably, or send love to Grandpa Phil. There is no voice in your head at those moments. Just peace, love, joy, sorrow, or whatever feeling the moment brings. As opposed to thinking, feeling represents your deepest experience of being alive.

And so, we reasoned, if your soul doesn't die and if feeling and life are one and the same, what's the big deal about also feeling some discomfort? It's not going to kill you. Why not say yes to life in all of its forms? "If you avoid your feelings," I told them, "you'll become at war with yourself, afraid of your shadow, afraid of pleasure too." As Bob Dylan wrote, "It frightens me, the awful truth, of how sweet life can be."

I asked the kids to examine their resistance to feeling pleasure and the fear of "losing one's self" in the bliss of the moment as well as being aware of their resistance to feeling disturbing feelings like anger, sadness, and such.

You can't choose to feel just fun stuff and push away the painful feelings because the system doesn't work like that. "The degree to which you are willing to feel pain is in direct proportion to your ability to feel pleasure," Eva Peirakkos writes in her book *Guide Lectures for Self-Transformation.*

This lesson was seared into my own soul by a dog name Jim. I got him when I was 29-years-old, a few months after Marko died. Jimmy was a Shepherd mix, a savvy stray that looked both ways before crossing the street and always had a gaggle of new friends around him. To say that we were inseparable is an epic understatement. Even a trip to the dry cleaner might give rise to feelings of separation anxiety. After seven years together, we had knee surgery the same week. Three years after that, he came down with lung cancer a month after I got my cancer diagnosis, and I wonder if Jimmy somehow sucked the disease out of me so that I might live. When it came time to lay him to rest, I was three months into chemotherapy and digging his grave in the backyard of our home in Boulder. Pick and shovel. Sweat and tears. Nancy Griffith's *"Great Divide"* played on the patio speakers as Jim sat on the grass watching me, a knowing look in his eyes. Our time had come. A few hours later, the digging done, the vet came and Jim had a final bowl of chocolate ice cream, a last hug and scratch of his ears.

The feelings I had while tossing dirt on my dear, sweet friend's grave that evening ranged from anguish to surprising joy at having known such tender and unconditional love. I had never experienced such pain, sorrow, and inexplicable happiness. I cried for myself, wailed for Jimmy, and for a thousand lifetimes of welled up grief. And by doing so, I felt deeply alive.

Your Brother Thinks You're a Douche

I asked my boys to embrace their feelings, and I also asked them to learn to take responsibility for their lives and not blame others for how they feel. Of course, this was an ongoing process, a lesson that took years to learn.

When the boys were little, they occasionally lacked impulse control, unable to be kind to each other. One of Alice's techniques was to redirect their behavior. She made them sit on the sofa and they couldn't get up until they said something nice to each other. On one occasion at the age of four, perplexed, grasping for something kind to say about his big brother, Josh finally offered that, "Jackson's farts smelled good."

The last time I spoke to them on the subject of sibling kindness was one day when they were about 6- and 8-years-old—each was convinced his brother was a total douche. I sat them down and reminded them that we all inherently want to do whatever is to our own benefit, and we can start by being aware of what's real now.

Then I posed a question to them both, "Exactly how is it to your benefit for your brother to think you're a total a-hole? How is it to your benefit for him to have a festering, brooding resentment towards you? Could you please explain that to me?" This question was initially met with silence.

"But Jackson is so annoying!"

"So what's your objection to feeling annoyed?" This question was met with laughter.

"Stop with the story in your head about how you're a victim. The victim/victimizer trap is like quicksand. Stop digging a deeper hole. Take responsibility for your experience. Step into the flow of your life. Put up and shut up," I said. "Stop imagining yourself a victim and stop being a victimizer. You can't feel like one without also being the other. This is the energetic fact of the matter.

"When you're having a little trouble with your brother (or anyone else), ask yourself, 'What's the truth of the matter?' and you'll probably see that you played some role in perpetuating the conflict. Let go of your need to be right, to be heard, to be understood.

"If you continue being unkind to each other, later in life you may not have a close relationship. For a time, I knew this with my own brother. There are consequences later due to your actions now. Once your mom and I are gone, your brother may be your only close family member, and wouldn't it be a shame if you weren't tight because you were unable to be kind when you were kids?"

(*And especially don't blame your brother if the* **asparagus vinaigrette** *disappears before you've had your fair share.*)

My friend Jordan says that managing reactivity is your "response-ability"—exercising your ability to respond.

She says, "I don't have to do the same thing over and over. I don't have to close my eyes in fear when the baseball comes. I can learn to respond differently—to keep my eyes open, step aside, and 'clunk,' the ball lands in my mitt."

Authenticity

"I was just too stubborn to ever be governed by enforced insanity, someone had to reach for the rising stars, I guess it was up to me," Dylan again from *"Up To Me"*, a brilliant reminder for us all to be authentic, follow our passions, and not organize life around what others may think.

When Jackson was 17-years-old and applying to schools, Deep Springs College in California asked him for several additional essays since he had made it through the first round cut. The required essay topics included doing something challenging, something he hadn't done before, and then writing about it. He first thought about physical feats like hiking our beloved Red Lady Mountain at dusk, the peak that shadows our town, and then skiing down in the moonlight.

Standing face to face with him in the kitchen that January morning, I suggested challenging himself in a different way. "Explore your vulnerability. Act on the truth of how you feel when it's scary, raw, naked. That's true strength." I knew there was a woman (I can't call her a girl because she's ten years older than Jackson) that he had a mad crush on and I suggested that he tell her. "Practice radical authenticity and let the chips fall as they may. Let go of control, embrace how you feel without expectation and see where the day takes you. You might be pleasantly surprised, or deeply disappointed. But you'll know true strength and tenderness for self. This is the way of the ancient heroes."

Terrified, Jackson took my advice. He even wrote her a song which he played on the guitar and sang to her over a candlelit lunch of leek fritters and arugula salad he prepared. Later, this experience did become one of the Deep Springs essays. He also reports that he's continued to develop a sweet and tender friendship with Madame X.

Here's an excerpt from Jackson's essay:

The difficulty was to see all the self-perpetuated obstacles aimed at avoiding feelings of vulnerability as the illusions they are. I feared being mocked, making a fool of myself, and having the song not be to her taste. Essentially, I feared my dick would be too small and I would get laughed at. To transcend these difficulties required immediacy, radical authenticity, non-attachment, surrender to feeling, and genuine Love, making raising my voice quite challenging.

The challenge didn't end with the first awkward note. I noticed well into the second verse I wasn't making eye contact with her so in that moment, the challenge was to look her in the eye, which I did. Eye contact made me even more naked. My heart was quaking as my eyes were seeing her seeing me seeing the beauty in her. We were making love. The tender innocence was crushing yet invigorating. The experience can only be talked about poetically, over-intellectualization only kills the raw feelings that were expressed. My head was the biggest hurdle I had to step over; it seems impossible to be vulnerable from the head.

Only the heart knows the immortality that dwells within mortality.

By no longer identifying with the part of my self that fears vulnerability, I challenged the validity of those pre-existing fears. The challenge was to challenge a way I often operate. Most people's difficulties are an internal conflict between the self working to avoid disturbance and the deeper being's intrinsic momentum to grow and celebrate life, which involves disturbance. A challenge is any undertaking of actively rejoining the whole being with its deeper movements of growth and celebration. In singing my song, I was paying tribute, celebrating life and surrendering to growth.

(*You can try some of Jackson's* **leek fritters** *yourself, ripped off from the hit cookbook "Plenty"*).

I was impressed with the way he let it all hang out and he continues to challenge himself to lead a life on the wild side. Yet, on the other hand, it can also be to your benefit to apply some restraint in your pursuit of authenticity.

I remember when Josh was about ten, getting in trouble at school for entertaining his friends with his legendary sense of humor. On this particular occasion, I believe he was sent to the principal's office for addressing his attractive young teacher as "toots," a word I'd perhaps last heard spoken by my grandfather some forty years past. I told him, "If you look to others for your identity, to feel good about yourself, you forfeit your personal power and become dependent upon the whims of others. This is a prescription for anxiety that gets automatically refilled. Even if you get positive reinforcement, like an addict, you're always in need of the next fix, confirmation from others that you exist. And by the way, how could it possibly be to your benefit for me to get a call from the principal? Could you please explain that to me?" As expected, this question was met with silence.

"Instead, rest in your Greater Nature and laugh at your need for validation from others, appreciate the perfection of the moment while still allowing for your individual and odd choices like wearing shorts all winter or parading around like "Lil' M" [Josh's rap star alter-ego so designated by Jackson upon seeing him in a particular white hat and hoodie combination]. As Michael Franti sings, 'All the freaky people make the beauty of the world,' but he didn't say it was okay to disrespect your teachers and disrupt your fellow students."

I also told him that he would miss his beloved hockey season if these lapses in judgment continued. A call from the principal for any reason, even if he were falsely accused, would cause an immediate suspension of at least one league game. And I also decreed that Josh needed to maintain a beefier GPA in order to continue playing hockey. He knew I wasn't joking and now Josh had my line of reasoning and the traction to successfully manage his behavior *and* his studies.

His seemingly humble response to this diatribe was, "I hear you, Dad. You should really write a book." And while I've taken Josh's advice, I was perhaps a bit too pleased with his suggestion. I'm reminded of the character played by Dwight Yokam, the hapless husband at the mercy of divorce mediators Owen Wilson and Vince Vaughn, in the opening scene of *Wedding Crashers*—ultimately, his only request of them was to, "Please stop talking."

While writing this book, I told Josh that I'd mentioned the "toots incident" and also included a vignette on when he was a chubby adolescent, not yet grown into his frame—how I made the classic parenting mistake of projecting my own fears onto him. He demanded editorial review if not a full retraction of both stories. I told him my information on the "toots incident" came from Bob (the enforcer at school), and that Josh should direct any complaints to him. I quoted the masthead on *The Aspen Daily News*, "If you don't want to read about it, don't let it happen." I declined to omit the story and somewhat sarcastically announced, "Feel free to write your own book." Without missing a beat, he said, "Yeah, and it's gonna be called *Richard, the Asshole*."

I laughed, and in an effort to distance myself from his memoir replied, "How about *Dick, The Asshole?* That's catchier." Josh said, "YEAH! THAT'S IT!!! *DICK, THE ASSHOLE!!!*" We burst out laughing and the look on his face was sheer delight. I told Josh that if he insists, I would omit the story about my parenting mistake with his pre-pubescent weight gain but just think of how many kids could be helped if parents can learn to be more skillful. He thought about it and said it'd be okay—look for more on this story later in the book.

(*Josh's favorite* **chicken in a skillet** *can also be used as bribery.*)

Remember When You Were the Mountain

Whether you're a parent or child, in the world of feelings things just *are*. By being willing to feel pain and pleasure in equal measure you'll eventually see the irony in both—pleasure has the seeds of pain, as good times are fleeting, and pain has the seeds of pleasure, as it's a wake-up call to aliveness. By practicing equanimity, there is no fear of what life may bring next and the result is a sense of Spaciousness. Peace is your baseline sensation, alertness your natural state.

When we accept life as it is in this moment, we stop suffering. We might feel pain, yes, from grief to anger to whatever, but it won't be suffering that you're vainly wishing away. As I learned when I had cancer, resistance to pain invites true suffering because you attach a time value to it, viewing your pain through the past or the future, while avoiding the raw feeling, the truth of the moment.

Looking at it from the perspective of a cyclist is helpful. Imagine being on a long hard ride, wondering when it will be over, wishing you hadn't gone so hard on that last hill, wondering when the ride will be over, instead of marveling at how much your legs hurt now. And now. And now.

What I've discovered is that there is space in between the

agony, and the pain doesn't hurt at that instant. If I'm super skillful, I express gratitude and retain my fascination for every moment. Even an amazing display of pain is sacred. Holy Shit!!!

Viewed with kindness and openness toward all states of being, pain becomes just another feeling. It becomes tolerable, even funny how intense it can be. By approaching life as theater, knowing that the only certainty is change, the laws of impermanence irrefutable, we can playfully experience intensity knowing it won't last. In fact, it may get even "worse" . . . or it may resolve in a surprising way.

When I was going through chemotherapy, I remember one particular evening—I was lying in bed around midnight, my stomach bloated like a toad. I was curled up in the fetal position, and the prescription meds for nausea didn't help. I finally prayed, "Please God, help me with this pain in my belly." What happened next was right out of a movie. About a foot in front of my eyes I saw a ticker tape scroll across my field of vision with only the word TUMS. I thought, "You've got to be kidding. I must be hallucinating." But it was an apparition too strong to ignore. I got myself dressed, drove to the 24-hour supermarket, and in the aisle chewed up a half dozen Tums tablets. INSTANTLY I felt better. The pain in my stomach went from a ten to a two. You might think that I made this story up, but you'd be wrong. Sometimes our prayers are answered, and whether it's our body, emotions or apparitions, as we participate we allow for the possibility of being pleasantly surprised.

When you witness a repetitive story going on in your head, ask yourself, "What is the underlying feeling that I'm avoiding?" Let go of the story and give yourself permission to experience the raw vulnerability. Ask, "What's my objection to feeling [the dreaded emotional display]?" Close your eyes for one minute and give yourself permission to experience the raw fear, anger, sadness, anxiety, or whatever the avoided feeling might be.

Let go of the idea that you're angry because the dishes aren't done. Instead, acknowledge, "I think I'm avoiding anger." Without blaming anyone for how you feel, acknowledge that the kitchen doesn't look the way you'd like and give yourself permission to just feel angry. Close your eyes and be as angry as you can for 60 seconds—the most angry person that's ever lived. To do this for a full minute is nearly impossible, as you'll probably just burst out laughing after 20 seconds. Give yourself permission to feel and it passes. It doesn't matter if the dishes get done this second or not. The emotional display will move out with the tide when it's not avoided. And perhaps this entire process will need to be repeated again in five minutes. Lather. Rinse. Repeat.

Reclaim your avoided feelings and be whole, otherwise your disowned pain will run you like the tail that wags the dog. You'll be continually anxious and this will surface in ever more insidious ways, like the child who throws tantrums and doesn't even know why. If you own all your feelings, your life will transform. You'll no longer be at war with yourself. It works. This practice works for kids, too.

My friend Jordan was a school counselor and she told me a story about a first-grader she encountered who was facing a corner in the hallway and sobbing uncontrollably. She took him into her office and each time he began to quiet down she tried to kindly and helpfully ask some version of, "What's going on?" He would then begin sobbing all over again. This went on five times until finally he was composed enough to answer, "I don't remember." Jordan checked back with his teacher and she reported that after that day, he was much more focused, a better student. And while it works for a first-grader to burst into tears in the hallway, as an adult you can politely excuse yourself to experience the truth of your being too. Scream into a pillow. Cry in your bedroom. You too may be more focused if you reclaim the disowned aspects of your self. It doesn't matter *"why"* you are having feelings, just that you *are* feeling.

If you're unclear what you're feeling, ask simply, "What am I feeling now?" Or possibly, "What am I avoiding feeling now?"

As you welcome your feelings with equanimity and participate in them without judgment, the reward for your bravery and honesty will be an abiding sense of security and ease; you will develop a new resilience that allows you to keep your heart truly open without getting sucked into drama. You develop compassion and tenderness without neediness or neurotic co-dependency.

Bubbling aliveness will result when you earnestly search for the truth of what you are feeling. You'll become intimately familiar with your natural orientation towards spaciousness, alertness, and peace.

Be brave enough to share your truth with the world and see where the day takes you. "Being authentic will always connect you to the moment," wrote Eva Peirrakos. "You will experience vibrancy, aliveness, and the free flow of love as you connect with your creative force. You're able to breathe, relax, and let down your guard. Choosing to actively welcome your raw feelings and vulnerabilities can be scary, but you'll always come to the same conclusion: It's safe to be you . . . [and] as you reveal the truth of yourself to the world, you purify your own soul. For it is only the purified soul that can stand long in the blinding current of divine love. This is what we fear and yearn for most." Be extreme. Surrender to the bliss of being truly authentic. Truly present. Truly alive. This is your birthright.

As you lovingly tend to both the weeds and flowers of your garden, allowing the sun to shine brightly on your fears and desires, you gain confidence. You realize that it's all good. You realize there is never a reason to fear being authentic any more than the mountain or river could be embarrassed by what they are.

Be gentle with yourself as you grow. The philosopher Alan Watts said, "Enlightenment isn't a state of mind but a kindness towards all states of mind." Why not let go of the story and feel the vulnerability you seek to avoid by complaining? Remember when you were the mountain.

The psychologist Bruce Tift wrote that, "As we expand our identity to the whole nature of life, embracing the perspective that self is an illusion, we know we can't be threatened. There is nothing that has a separate existence that can be threatened by life."

If you can make the leap of faith to believe it, or better yet, feel it, then you'll have your liberation. As Tift notes, "This perspective won't dissolve pain but it will eliminate chronic anxiety and paranoia" as you no longer struggle through life resisting and wishing it was different.

I know some of this is pretty heady stuff but with a bit of explanation and discussion, a bit of patience and practice, kids may acquire an active understanding of immediacy, aliveness, and awareness at a surprisingly early age. Maybe they'll even get it before you do. Maybe start with a bedtime story:

When I was the stream, when I was the forest, when I was every foot, fin and wing, when I was the sky, no one ever asked me did I have a purpose, no one wondered was there anything I might need, for there was nothing I could not love. It was when I left all that we once were that the agony began, the fear and questions came and I wept tears I'd never known before. So I returned to the river, I returned to the mountain, I again asked for their hand in marriage. I begged to marry every object and creature; and when they accepted, God was ever present; and he did not say, "Where have you been?" For then I knew my soul, every soul, has always held him.

~ 13th century Christian Monk, Meister Eckhart

Work To Survive

As kids do dishes, they'll see their reflection. If they wash with love, they'll feel peaceful. They may even wash with delirious ecstasy, maniacally devoted to the moment, anxious only to move on to the counters and floors. Or if they're uninspired by their soapy sink and wishing they weren't washing, they might suffer like a dog in the cold, and that's okay too. At the very least, they'll learn to manage their discomfort, building strength and resilience. Jackson reports that he occasionally washes while feeling a broad range of emotions—anger that Josh and I don't do our share, desire for approval, to be in service, or sacred communion with the cups and plates that hold our daily bread (presumably, his preferred approach). Josh scores points for honesty as he reports feeling "this sucks" while cleaning the kitchen, wondering what he might get out of me for doing it.

Why dishes? For starters, splashing around in the water is fun. It's an entry-level position and your toddler can begin on a stepstool. A two-year-old can play at the sink, a five-year-old can do it with your supervision, and a seven-year-old can do it on their own. In some countries, kids herd sheep at the age of five and play an important role in the family's economic health. "Hey! How 'bout herding that pile of laundry?"

Your kids have the dexterity and intelligence to contribute. They are considerably more agile and smarter than your house pet. What they lack is training and focus. You'll be shocked by what they're capable of and the pleasure they may take in being helpful. Assign them tasks that YOU want done. All you have to do is train them properly, make an effort to keep them accountable, and tell them thanks every day, how much you appreciate all that they do. Ask them, "How does it feel to be so helpful and independent?" Tell them how good it makes you feel. Catch them being good.

You might explain how Daddy and Mommy work to provide for the family and that by doing dishes, folding laundry, helping out around the house, they are contributing and participating in an important way, too. They learn gratitude and appreciation for their good fortune, the food, warm clothes, their parents who love them, and the innate satisfaction that comes from completing a job well done.

When they are actively engaged in the welfare of the household, kids align themselves with universal forces that celebrate gratitude and service. Doing dishes together may also provide a casual forum to discuss this 'n that.

I told my kids that we're all individual carbon life forms, and in a cosmic sense, no more significant than the average insect buzzing about. And buzz as we may, every carbon life form must work to survive. If you're not willing to work to perpetuate your gift of life, then you're in for a rude awakening. If you feel entitled to life, you're going to be at odds with the dirty dishes in the sink and you're going to be at odds with everything else, including and especially yourself.

I once even suggested to my boys, "If you're too little to get a job at the railroad to help pay the rent, you must find some other tribute. You might trade a goat or a hen. Or if you're a kid without a goat, you can provide a service." By aligning their habits with service and gratitude, their values will develop accordingly. It actually feels good to be helpful and express thanks. Eventually, they may cheerfully do just about any mundane task, which feels nice for everyone.

"Hey, would you mind feeding Mookie and filling his water dish?"

[Author's note: Mookie is a portugese water dog that fully embraces our small town lifestyle and his days are replete with independent walkabouts, random belly rubs and a casual patrol for the as yet undiscovered, perfect porch for napping. Crested Butte is ripe with summer vacation renters and it's not unusual to get a phone call that starts with, "Ummm...excuse me, but I think your dog is asleep on my sofa." Mookie is an unrepentant freeloader and the sole exception in our work to survive manifesto.]

Shut the Fuck Up

Do you go the extra mile because it makes you feel needed somehow or perhaps because it speaks to your identity as a "good parent"? Obviously, you provide for your kids because you love and care for them, but every day with your kids can also be a day to teach them independence and offer them the freedom to grow, to be creative, and learn to take responsibility for their own life. Your family is a laboratory. Feel free to experiment. You may want to start by considering what kind of behavior you are modeling and what kind of creatures are currently growing in the petri dish you call home.

If you teach kids to listen to themselves in real time and make decisions on their own, whatever their situation may be, then I think you've done your job as a parent. By coddling or micro-managing your kid, you may be feeding your own ego, energizing your fears, and actually preventing your kids from becoming self-actualized and independent beings. By being over-involved, you undermine their confidence and limit their potential for future happiness and success. You may be caught up in a neurotic web of codependency, perhaps not unlike the dysfunction many experience with their spouse or significant other.

Why not let go of worrying about what your kids need

next? You're not ultimately in control anyway. As I told Robin that morning, the future will take care of itself in the most delightful ways (think The Sound of Music) if you can learn to let go of your agenda and simply shut the fuck up. Sorry, but that's what it took for Robin to hear me. I also told her that her kids often experienced her as being a fucking bitch due to her nagging and asked how that could possibly be to her benefit.

I don't normally speak like that and said it to her most unexpectedly and quite cheerfully.I said it for shock value and to add emphasis to my petition. Robin was rightly offended, but it was shortly thereafter that she had her epiphany.

I agonized over including this phrase as I know it will offend some kindly readers though it seems to me that it's only this kind of vulgarity that adequately speaks to the obscene practice of bossing your kid around as if you knew what your kid needs to do or think. Micro-managing your kid is deeply offensive and a huge spiritual, emotional and practical mistake. I know, because I made it with Josh. I also decided to include the above as something of a litmus test: If you don't see any wisdom in my salty suggestion, then like my dear, sweet friend Robin, this section was written justly for you.

When I was between the ages of ten and thirteen, I was chubby and this was very painful for me. It affected my self-esteem and kids teased me. When Josh began to gain extra weight at a similar age, I projected my own experience onto him. I cajoled him to eat healthy and get more exercise and badgered Alice to provide low-sugar, low fat, healthy food at her house. If he wanted dessert, I might give him a questioning look of disapproval. He resented me.

He became self-conscious. He thought I was a dick. I knew it was wrong of me yet I couldn't control myself. I even told him at the time why it was such a charged issue for me, but it was no excuse for my boorish behavior.

Eventually, Josh received a lecture from his hockey coach to get in better shape, which he did, and this year Josh's hockey team made it to the state championship. Josh has forgiven me for not having successfully managed my own unresolved pain and I love him all the more for his open heart. He understands my humanness and the parenting mistakes I've made because of it. I wish I'd stayed out of his face and allowed him to grow at his own pace.

Instead of being bossy, feel the vulnerability you seek to avoid by complaining and controlling. Give yourself a hug. Give your kid a hug. Shut the fuck up! Like Josh, your kid doesn't need fixing.

(*Instead, fix 'em* **Brussell Sprouts** *made famous at Alta in New York City and deftly executed at Django's in Crested Butte—nobody at my house would complain.*)

Robin now wears an unusual bracelet to remind herself to chill out. She says, "I've taken to wearing a horrendous bracelet made of fluorescent beads—a nuclear warning system on my wrist as a reminder to stay vigilant at not telling them what to do and managing my reactivity. I don't wear it every day, but it's always on the dresser, a hideous reminder . . . to give up the control. That's the bottom line. I've just chosen in the last month to do things differently, to say things a little differently. If it's not on my timetable, it's ok, it gets done. With the changing of my language and giving up that things have to be my way, my life has changed dramatically for the better. Last week, I was asked if this practice had changed anything with my husband, and that same day I went home and everything was done. The bathroom was clean, the dishes were done, the house swept and vacuumed. I was almost in shock." Alternatively, you could wear a rubber band on your wrist and snap it before foolishly snapping at someone else.

Boundaries and Consequences

Robin's transformation came when she made a decision to lighten up with her twin 10-year-old boys—after which she "witnessed the beauty of the death of control." Instead of nagging them to do their homework when they got home from school, she lets them get it done on their own schedule and suffer the consequences if their grades slip (which they haven't). She used to clean her boys' room because she couldn't stand for it to not be done the way she liked (personally, I don't care if my boys' room is a disaster, provided that they respect the common areas of the house). Robin reports that life has become *beautiful* since she let go of her need for control:

"I was never really in control but I was trying. And it was making me crazy because the floor wasn't swept the way I would've liked or it wasn't on my timetable. I changed from saying, 'Put your dish in the dishwasher,' to 'I'm so happy when you put your dish in the dishwasher.' And after three days of saying, 'It makes me feel great,' and 'It makes me feel happy,' they're now doing it on their own. There's no more struggle. It's amazing. Why was I being so militant? Just change the language and give up the control. It led to other things like, 'There's a whole sink filled with of dishes. It would make Mom so happy if I did those.'"

If you do feel strongly about an issue, keep a good boundary for yourself and cheerfully offer a consequence instead. It's important to note that a key part of Robin's transformation with the twins included the introduction of significant consequences in order to get her kids attention, to let them know she was serious.

"From now on," said Robin, "take your dishes to the sink after dinner every night *without me asking* or there's no skiing this weekend."

Keep good boundaries around what is and isn't acceptable to you, and at the same time play with your own discomfort that the house is a noisy mess. Allow others to be in their own creative flow. "Be careful not to interrupt" is my motto.

Wanna bang the drum all afternoon? Okay, I guess. That is, until I just can't take it anymore, at which point I ask myself, "What's my objection to feeling so disturbed now? Maybe I could give it another minute?" And then returning to those questions over and over if necessary. Often, just as I'm about to throw in the towel, the drum would be put down and they'd move on to something incrementally less annoying.

If you're feeling reactive, it's a signal you aren't being kind enough to self and haven't enforced proper boundaries. Or it could be that you aren't adequately managing your discomfort. Only you know how you feel in the moment and what the situation calls for.

The first boundary that I recall enforcing was "no whining." Ask me once, no problem. Ask me again, and the answer is still no. "Hey—could you please not ask me again. And if you do ask me again, I'm not going to take you and your friends swimming this afternoon." Ask me that third time and there will be the promised consequence that was cheerfully suggested upon the second petition. It might be the removal of a favorite toy or the cancellation of an activity. I kept my tone light even while I threatened consequences that would be draconian, diabolical, and designed to inflict immediate age-appropriate hardship. And I followed through.

To be clear, there was no *schadenfreude* at play. I took no pleasure in their pain. I was simply hyper-vigilant at insuring that my boys got the message: They were not in control of my demeanor or my feelings. I intended to remain cheerful regardless of their choices and remind them that they did not possess the power to ruin *my* day, only theirs.

Setting consequences like this made my expectation clear. They would respect my boundaries just as I vowed to respect theirs (even before they were born). They knew I wouldn't cave and they would suffer. The whining was just not an option for them.

I also placed limits on the time spent on television, video games, and other vacuous, sedentary, mindless crap. Though I had to be careful of the behavior I modeled as I'm a bit more like Josh, happy to zone out in front of the television or computer at night. When the boys were little, my secret pleasure was watching American Idol, and Josh and I would beg Jackson to watch with us, physically restraining him on the sofa as we laughed and tickled our way through the theme song.

Independence

Do you organize your kid's time? I'd rather my boys decide for themselves what activities they want to participate in and who their friends should be.

Consider the four-year-old who gets dressed in the morning with the shirt on backwards and shoes on the wrong feet. Instead of taking charge or criticizing them, take a moment to praise them for their independence. Eventually, they'll figure out that their feet hurt and make the switch themselves. Or you could gently introduce the idea a bit later that morning.

When Jackson was twelve, he began spending time with Marcie, a 60-year-old local storyteller. I occasionally asked what they discussed but didn't pry. He seemed to gain something from his visits, and while I was curious to know more, I trusted him to follow his own path and didn't push him to share more than he cared to.

When Jackson was 14, he announced that he wanted to take a semester off of school and travel to the Middle East and Europe on his own. He felt stifled from having been in school for almost ten years and he wanted to experience more of the world while he was still young. He fancied himself a burgeoning poet and he claimed it essential to the development of his art that he have this experience.

Who was I to say no?

I know, his father!

But, he'd saved his money from summer jobs for the trip and made plans to live there for three months. With great reluctance, I said yes to his proposal, knowing our family had friends and contacts in various places in case of emergency. He was 15 when he left, and I had a clear image of him returning home safely, feathers ruffled, perhaps a bit humbler and wiser too. But to be fair, I also wondered if I was suppressing my own fear for his safety.

I said a prayer for my boy every day and Jackson says that by giving him extraordinary freedom, the world became his teacher. By not needing to know everything he was exposed to every minute of the day, Jackson says that I allowed him "to develop an intimate relationship with the world, and allow life to be his parent." This might be an extreme example, but I've observed my kids become more skillful at solving problems on their own as a result of my respecting their independence and sovereignty.

Sovereignty

On most days, I feel as though my boys and I are caught up in an unusual and extraordinarily loving domestic partnership—a divine union of sovereign beings, a comedy of equals. I figure that they alone know their true blueprint for happiness. My most important job is to create a safe place where they can remember their divine imprint and allow it to bubble up without any drama from me.

I discovered how to offer up suggestions that respected their sovereignty and, paradoxically, I may have had an even greater influence on them because I offered my opinions respectfully. I've given up the idea that they'll always listen to me and I have confidence that they're capable of running their own lives.

As sovereign beings, we have a trade agreement and a security pact, though mostly we have an emotional and spiritual treaty that allows us to feel safe, supported, and free to be authentic.

This is a two-way street as I also let down my guard and share details of my life that are both disturbing and pleasurable. I feel a sense of spaciousness and ease and don't feel like I have anything to hide or protect them from. When

I suffered a financial reversal several years ago, I was open with them and explained that our spending habits needed to change. And when my girlfriend and I broke up, I wasn't embarrassed to let them know how sad I was.

In addition to being a loving father, I consider myself a successful "family CEO," managing our scarce resources and teaching the kids to be cheerfully involved in the juggernaut of our joint enterprise. And as fate would have it, as if right on cue, as I write this I have just been handed a surprise gooey panini made by Josh. "Thanks! What, no chips?"

(Josh's **vegetarian panini** *recipe is not to be missed)*

Happily, we cater to each other, but we don't feel responsible for each other's happiness—and because of this healthy separation we may be able to offer true compassion and consistent kindness. We avoid control and encourage personal responsibility. We are curious and get to know each other. We ask a lot of questions. We don't demand. We care for each other, laugh at each other, and have been having fun together for longer than I can remember. As Michael Franti wrote, "Everyone deserves music." Everyone has their own song to sing.

I find it helpful to consider every person their own individual country with their own boundaries, language, customs and culture, and that the supreme ruler of this divine sovereign territory is them-self. By being diplomatic and considering others from a place of humility, you're able to develop and enjoy peaceful relations. You create the spaciousness to be compassionate without judgment or the need to fix anything.

My kids and I consider ourselves fellow students on the path of life, and even constructive criticism is unwelcome, a violation of the other's sovereignty. Unsolicited advice is generally received as criticism unless skillfully offered. This is the energetic fact of the matter.

Instead, ask for permission to give a suggestion: "May I give you my opinion on...?" This perspective slows you down a bit. And if they say no, sit with your own discomfort. As previously mentioned, shut the fuck up. Spiritually speaking, you don't have the right to tell kids (or anybody!) what they "should think" or "need to do." And if you do receive permission to offer an opinion, it could be phrased as, "I think it would be to your benefit to..."

It seems like a no-brainer, and in my house all of these beautiful, wonderful, unintended consequences occurred as a result of practicing radical personal sovereignty and requiring service. They got it. They quickly figured out that it feels good to pitch-in. It feels good to take responsibility for one's life experience.

If the right seeds are planted and a bit of water provided, there is no telling what might grow...

In 2005, a friend of mine, Brenda Fox, and I were talking one day about how Jackson and her daughter Ayanna (both 10-years-old) would enjoy meeting because of their shared approach to life. One of us suggested they get together and start an organization called "Conscious Kids." Jackson and Ayanna thought it was a good idea and they created a website for like-minded folk. They printed orange rubber bracelets with the Conscious Kids moniker, and a bunch of them are still sitting in a dusty box somewhere. While the organization did not manifest their wildest dreams, Jackson and Ayanna did organize several community service projects and affirm their beliefs in front of their peers. Perhaps they planted a few seeds of awareness among them, too.

Probably the most famous person to ever wear a Conscious Kids bracelet was Michael Franti, referred to by my friend Arthur as The Musical Dalai Lama. Franti was in Crested Butte to present his movie *I Know I'm Not Alone*, documenting his busking adventures through Baghdad and The Gaza Strip (Franti plays street music in for real war zones, spreading his singularly infectious badass love).

On behalf of Conscious Kids, Jackson wrote to Franti and invited him to speak to the students at the Crested Butte Community School when he was due in town. Franti graciously accepted and held the students and faculty transfixed with his presentation. He discussed his time in Gaza and Baghdad and then gave a solo acoustic performance. Even the most cynical was unable to suppress a smile.

It's never too early to talk to your kids about building community and taking responsibility for life, marching to their own beat and maybe spreading a bit o' love too. After seven years in a dusty box, Robin reminded me of Conscious Kids and suggested that we dig up the remaining bracelets and pass them out at Jackson's graduation party. A fitting tribute to the power of kids empowered.

Kids as Teachers

My belief is that kids are here to be your teachers and not the other way around. I don't mean they are here to be your guru though I've heard more than a few wise observations from my boys including the dreaded, "Dad, you seem a bit defensive."

I feel that having these wild cards in my life, these other people who were now my responsibility, provided a tremendous opportunity for self-realization. I thought that if I were to somehow allow their Divine Plan to unfold without my egoic imprint, then the entire process of raising kids might be infused with more grace and less stress. I thought it possible I might become more patient and kind. I hoped to set a good example, be a good listener and a trusted confidant. I feel humbled and blessed by them, and through them, I find it possible to open my heart to the Divine Flow in a whole new way.

I also believe that in some Wacky Way, kids actually choose their parents and owe their folks a measure of gratitude for hosting them. (Perhaps from the un-manifested world they say, "I'd like my soul to inhabit that fertilized egg." Or better, "I bet that guy can cook!"). We feed them, wipe their bottoms, work three shifts at the factory, let's face it—everyone benefits when kids challenge their status as freeloaders and are otherwise disabused of any misguided notions of victimhood.

"Sorry dude. You picked me."

My friend Arthur wonders if laziness has influenced my thinking in any way. This argument is not entirely without merit although I prefer to believe that I've done a nice job being a teacher and motivator over the years and am not a diabolical slacker bent on taking over the world one kid at a time. I've also learned that when you let them, kids can give us a nudge to follow our own path, even one with a few unexpected twists and turns...

In 1983, when I was 23-years-old I began to have this dream: I was walking up a stone path with gigantic jagged mountains in the background. An old lady was on her way down and I asked, "Where are we?" "La-dock" she replied. I continued up the path to a large white building and then the dream ends.

After the third or fourth time having the same dream, I mentioned it to my friend Ivan Ussach and he was amazed. Ivan knew that Ladakh is a real place in northern India, a place where Tibetan culture and Buddhism has run uninterrupted for nearly a thousand years. I was in shock. I'd figured it was some made up name. Gibberish. I thought it'd be cool to visit one day.

The dreams stopped after I spoke to Ivan that night and the experience faded from my memory. Then, 17 years later, I was 40 years old, in the throes of cancer treatment, and at a yoga class with my friend Dr. Cynthia Ruggero. We were at Mahmood's house in Boulder, Colorado where he taught every

Friday morning and served tea and snacks afterward.

After class I went to use the bathroom, where there was a photograph I instantly recognized as the mountains from my dream. I hadn't thought of Ladakh since Ivan had told me about it and in typical slacker fashion, had not investigated further. Now suddenly, there they were.

I asked Mahmood if the picture had been taken in Ladakh. He seemed surprised.

"Yes! Have you been there?"

I told Cynthia and Mahmood the story of the recurring dream. Though busy with cancer treatment, I vowed to one day make my way to Ladakh.

Seven years later, I was telling the story to the kids, and Jackson—who was about twelve at that time—became quite interested in the subject. He even did a little research on it and discovered that Ladakh was also referred to as Little Tibet, with active and beautifully preserved Tibetan Buddhist monasteries and culture due to its remoteness and extraordinary good fortune.

Jackson looked for the mountains from my dream and over a period of a few months presented me with picture after picture of mountains and monasteries. Monasteries and mountains. Each time I wanted to say, "Yes, that's it." But I couldn't. Until I saw a picture of Lamayuru—I instantly recognized the image. It turned out Lamayuru was the oldest monastery in Ladakh, founded by Naropa in 1050. Jackson made me promise to take him and four months later we were off to India (Josh didn't want to go until a week before our departure when it was too late to get him a visa).

Upon our arrival in Ladakh we began visiting a monastery each day, traveling by car and hiking too. It was late May, the wild apricot blossoms were in full force, and the tourists had not yet arrived. It felt as if we had all of Ladakh to ourselves.

Now keep in mind, we had no set itinerary and had not made any advance arrangements (there are over fifty monasteries in Ladakh and we planned to see eight or ten—it's a big region). Not a lot of English is spoken in Ladakh and we just showed up wherever, whenever, saving Lamayuru for the end of our journey. We were greeted at each monastery by a boy monk, typically ten-years-old, and given a brief, polite tour though they seemed mostly bored by our presence.

But at Lamayuru, a Senior Lama met us at the front gates and put white scarves around our necks, a traditional gesture of welcome and respect. He ushered us into the private study of the Head Lama of Ladakh who just happened to be visiting that day and the next. The Head Lama invited us to sit with him in his private office while he recited prayers and practiced for a teaching he was to deliver the next day. We were served tea and snacks and treated like visiting dignitaries while Lamas continually scurried around to fill our cups and bring more food.

Jackson and I exchanged silent, knowing looks with each other. Later that afternoon we were given a grand tour of the monastery by a few of the Lamas. We sat in the Lamas' private meditation room overlooking the Zanskar Mountains. We were invited to relax. We were shown the hidden rooms of the monastery and even viewed Naropa's relics. We were served more food and drink and invited to stay the night.

Our experience at Lamayuru was a stark contrast to our

visits to the other monasteries. It felt like coming home. And without Jackson's nudge to go to Ladakh, I might have fallen prey to my own laziness and missed an amazing chapter in my life.

The Kindly Benevolent Sheriff

The practice of respecting your kid's sovereignty may tug at your heartstrings and sensibilities. You see your kid engaging in a behavior that is going to be painful for him, but you learn to keep your mouth shut as long as it isn't an issue of safety.

At age 10, Josh wanted to wear shorts to school every day through the winter snow, ice, and wind of Crested Butte (elevation 8,885 feet above sea level) which struck me as utterly ridiculous, though I consented since it was his balls that were going to freeze, not mine. Wardrobe choices, activities, free time, friends—it was all their call. I only interceded on matters of extreme personal safety.

Seeing Josh trundle off to school with bare pink knees, I at least convinced him to wear extra layers on top to keep his torso warm. I also told him that if he gets a cold or flu due to his stupidity that I wouldn't cater to him, bringing him cinnamon toast and chamomile tea with just a hint of lime. I wasn't going to fluff his pillows as he stayed home from school sick in bed. I promised him that it wasn't gonna be like that.

(*Though if you ARE home sick from school, you want to have on hand in the freezer,* **Robin's Chicken Soup** *made in the crock pot).*

Giving other people space and independence—even when they insist on doing things that seem utterly ridiculous—requires getting your own life together and skillfully managing your reactivity. Learning to do this is a lifelong process until, perhaps eventually, our emotional displays hold such little fascination that we barely chuckle at ourselves, like an old Seinfeld rerun we've seen too many times.

If this skill is not acquired, you (and your kid) may be the proverbial bull in a china shop—the entitled, outspoken, demanding, outrageous a-holes that unconsciously knock over the priceless Tiffany lamp without bothering to say you're sorry. So much for being invited to the super bowl party.

(Then again, if you brought **Spicy Fruit Salsa**, *you might wrangle an invitation anyway.)*

When I behave aggressively or reactively, I tend to take responsibility and apologize immediately. This act of self-awareness seems crucial. Apologizing to family members for antisocial behavior establishes a bond of trust and respect.

I believe that an enlightened CEO considers himself part of a team and wouldn't yell at his co-workers without saying he's sorry. My policy is that nobody gets a free pass for reactive behavior, including and especially me. So, establish terra firma. Be transparent. Be aware of the disproportionate power you hold in your relationship with your kids. Look for the blind spots in your character—the places you are reluctant to grow.

If I had a dollar for every time I apologized for raising my voice to my kids, I'd have more than enough for a fancy night on the town, with real champagne. It's not fun to apologize, but it lightens the mood, keeps me accountable and models self-awareness.

(*By the way, it's okay to delay your apology for a few minutes so as not to distract your kid from contemplating their role in the situation. That is, unless you were a total dick, in which case, you'd best apologize immediately and circle back to a heartfelt and intelligent discussion later.*)

If you do feel strongly about an issue, modify the kid's behavior by offering consequences instead of losing your temper. Think of yourself as the kindly benevolent sheriff, the sort that gets cats out of trees and walks old ladies across the street. A justice o' the peace. Not the type to bully a fellow citizen and only reluctantly slaps on the cuffs for a night in jail. And you'd rather the townsfolk work out their problems without the heavy hand o' the law.

I remember when I was about six-years-old being given a spanking for something I hadn't done. Between whacks on my butt, I recalled a few things that I had done wrong but hadn't been punished for. Was this the law of attraction that I now hear so much about? Or was my little brain just trying to make sense of something senseless?

If I got teary about something, my Dad would warn me, "I'll give you something to cry about." Predictably, I learned to go numb. I love my Dad and fear hurting his feelings by telling this story, though the reason I do so is as a cautionary tale. No matter how much you love your kids, if you don't manage your reactivity and unconsciously bully them, they will remember that as much as the love you give.

There is no excuse to yell at another human being any more than a country has the right to plant their flag in the land of another. When you yell at someone, you invade their personal space. It's an energetic act of war.

I suspect that frequent yelling activates an energetic field in your kid that turns on fear receptors, so that when you're merely near them they live on the edge, wary of your next outburst. But if you are self-reflective and apologize for your antisocial behavior in real-time, these receptors can heal in the moment. Trust and equilibrium can be restored.

Though my Dad undoubtedly loved me and did many wonderful things for me, it wasn't until I was well into adulthood that I could totally relax around him and fully enjoy his company, mature enough to no longer take anything personally.

If you're feeling reactive, it's always a sign that you're not being kind enough to yourself. How could it possibly be to your benefit to scream or yell at anyone? Who cares if they deserved it—yelling isn't going to stop the puppy from pooping in the kitchen. Cheerfully put it in a crate. Take it for a walk. Have a talk.

Life Isn't Fair

Life isn't fair, it just *is*. If you respect your own sovereignty, take responsibility for how you feel, then you'll break the cycle of blame and instead operate from a position of awareness and kindness towards self and others. You'll face the truth of how you feel and let go of the fantasy that life should be free from disturbance. Awareness of what you're feeling and the ability to manage those feelings without disrespecting others is a sign of your developing skill. This can't be taught too soon and it's never too late.

You become masterful and would never think to engage in an unkind word or a violent act merely because you're feeling angry now. Anger is part of being alive. No big deal. No need to blame anyone. And so, "you made me mad" gives way to, "I'm angry now." If someone else is mad, it's not your problem. This approach breaks the cycle of victim/victimizer.

When we become reactive, we are probably resisting some aspect of self that we don't wish to own up to, triggered by the other's behavior. Or maybe we're just judgmental and immature, thinking that everyone should see the "rightness" of our views. Investigate your emotional reactions. Be fearless with your self-examination. Give up your need to be right, to be heard, to be understood and escape the victim/victimizer trap.

Don't get me wrong here—how you feel may indeed be a consequence of someone else's actions, but the misconception is that you are a victim. No one is *making* you feel angry, you're just angry. This is a part of being alive. What's your objection to feeling the underlying anger? Why do you need to blame someone? Feel it and the anger will pass. Stew on the story and your whole life may pass.

Take responsibility for *your* feelings. People are entitled to *their* choices, opinions, and misconceptions no matter how ridiculous or cruel they may seem to you. Your choice is the company you keep, the behavior you model, and the boundaries you enforce for yourself.

You're under no obligation to associate with unconscious behavior. And if you should find this among a family member and he or she can't be avoided, then I suggest choosing to view them as your teacher in developing tolerance, patience, and compassion. Look to how you might be energizing the relationship with egoic behavior of your own. What's the truth of the matter?

(*And when I'm feeling reactive, **a smoothie** of pineapple, strawberry, ginger, and beet always cools me down. Shred the beets and ginger before you toss them in the blender, and obviously cut the skin off the pineapple and pluck the greens off the strawberry first too. Oh, and go easy on the beets and ginger. You can always add more to taste.*)

Empathy

"It begins with your family,
but soon it comes 'round to your soul."
~ Leonard Cohen, "Sisters of Mercy"

If my boy is having a tough day, I'll hopefully notice and check in with how he's feeling. I'll invite him to share, but I won't try to solve his problem. Instead, I'll acknowledge how he feels. Just be with him and listen, and if possible I'll share a story from my past that evoked a similar feeling in me. This simple act validates his feelings, so that he knows it's okay for him to feel the way he does.

It works wonders. For real.

Then possible courses of action may be tactfully discussed, or not. At least, I'll tell him I appreciate what he's feeling. *He needs a hug, not a solution.* And I'll continue to check in with how he's feeling throughout the day, but I won't take it personally. I will not agonize over his situation, rather I'll do my best to remain clear and empathetic, still happy to participate in my own day. My job is to live my life, not his.

[Author's Note: The practice of empathy can be successfully applied to all of your relationships. Acknowledge others' feelings without a need to fix anything. This method is beautifully articulated in Chaim Ginot's classic, *Between Parent and Child*. An easy and must read.]

We're All Working on Something

"I feel a mighty Judgment coming, but I may be wrong, you see you hear these funny voices in the tower of song."
~ Leonard Cohen, "The Tower of Song"

I sometimes prefer Josh's company because he's so easy going and entertaining. On the other hand, Jackson, now 17-years-old, can be overly discerning as to the spiritual and political correctness of others, which can make his company at times feel tedious, an energy suck. We all have our core issues to confront and Jackson willingly confesses that one of his issues is arrogance. Josh cheerfully acknowledges that one of his is laziness. Naturally, I suffer from both. We each do our best to be hyper-vigilant and kindly confront these reoccurring themes in our own lives while lovingly pointing them out in each other. As U.S. Supreme court Justice Benjamin Cordozo said, "Nothing sanitizes like sunlight."

Conscious Language

As Robin successfully learned, the most effective language with your kids is sincerely affirmative, "I love it when you do the dishes. It makes me feel great." In any life situation, talk about your feelings without expectation and see what happens. This approach motivates your kids to do the dishes without being told because they want to spread happiness and not just because you ask them. It feels good to give. Give them the space to be in the flow. Give them a gentle, skillful reminder when they're stuck.

I banished the words "need," "should," "trying," and "but" from my vocabulary and am cautious with "you," "why," "always," and "never."

Try rephrasing "You need to do the dishes" or "You should clean up your mess" with "I'd appreciate it if you did the dishes" or "You might consider doing the dishes." You can even make it a question, "So, when do you plan to clean up that mess?" Ask with non-attachment or you'll be spreading passive-aggressive vibes.

If you ever use the phrases like "You should..." or "You need to..." in a sentence, be very careful about what comes out next because you are not in charge of the other person.

Energetically, these words have presumptuous and aggressive overtones. They are sure to provoke resistance.

If it's *that* important that the kitchen gets cleaned up now, provide a consequence, which in effect respects their sovereignty and provides them a choice. "If you don't do the dishes now, you can forget about . . . "

Before using "you" in a sentence with anyone (not just your kids), substitute "I" for "you" in your head, and if you still like how the sentence sounds, continue apace. In reality, we're always talking about ourselves anyway, and the imagined shortcomings of others are really our own limitations and misconceptions that life should conform to our demands. Let your speech be uplifting. Or alternatively, you guessed it, shut the fuck up.

Be careful when you ask someone "why" they did this or that. It can have aggressive overtones and could be rephrased as, "Would you mind explaining to me your reasoning for?"

Instead of saying, "I love you, BUT you forgot to sweep," just say, "I love you AND you forgot to sweep." "But" tends to dismiss whatever came before it. Think about it.

Phrases that include "trying" and "can't" imply a state of victimhood, disempowerment, or a need for improvement. Accept who you are right now. Any change you *choose* to make *will* happen—you won't be *trying*, you'll be *doing*. If you say you're trying to quit smoking, you're really asking for pity without committing to quitting. You're a victim of your own weakness. In the world of energetic language, "trying" is failure and "can't" means won't. There is only doing and being.

When using the words "always" and "never," you are speaking in absolutes which are rarely correct and sure to provoke resistance to whatever you might have to say next.

Any time you use the word "should" in reference to yourself, try finishing the sentence in your head with, ". . . but I don't because I'm lame." When you say something like, "I should study," you're saying, "I know what's best for me and yet I'm not doing it." Substitute "could" for "should" and you'll inject a sense of spaciousness and truth into the conversation.

I doubt seriously that I will ever stop noticing a myriad of ways in which others might "improve," but I've learned to laugh at the folly of this voice in my head, and remind myself that everyone is on their own path. Why create drama by telling other people what they *should* think or *need* to do?

If you're precise with your language you'll have fewer arguments and more peace. Ask permission to give a suggestion. Have faith in the benevolent flow of life. All you can do is marvel at your kids, provide for them, teach them a few life skills and maybe learn a few new ones yourself.

Marko

Marko and I met ski bumming in Aspen in 1977, and briefly shared a trailer in Smuggler trailer court with our buddy Steve Scher. Steve, Marko, and I were all 18-years-old when we met that winter.

Marko was extraordinarily brilliant, charming, kind, and funny. We became business partners as well as best friends. One night in January 1988, when we were on a ski vacation in Vail, I woke up in the middle of the night screaming.

In my dream, I was holding a head in my hands. When I looked up, all I could see were feet standing way above me. I'd never had a nightmare before, but later that day, it went down exactly like that. Marko skied into a ravine and I came upon him seconds later. He was unconscious, his head crushed like an eggshell. I cradled his head, and when I looked up all I could see were the feet of the ski patrol above me at the top of the ravine. Marko was already gone. Finished his run.

After Marko's death, it was as if I could "feel him around." Once I thought I heard him whisper in my ear that if ever I should stumble, bump my knee, or whack my head that it was simply him saying hello.

Marko

When I told this story to my boys they felt a sense of wonder and amazement. My friend Kia elegantly accounts for the nonlinear nature of time by simply stating that "we're everywhere, always." Maybe Marko's story helped the boys feel safe to explore the supernatural phenomena of their own existence—to live in the moment and live for eternity.

Remember When You Were the River

So it went over the years, me doing my best Larry David impression, giving the kids broad latitude, and asking little in return except that they help out around the house, work to their potential in school, and offer kindness and respect to all. They seemed to trust me. Hopefully, they trust me most of all when I tell them I love them. And given the extraordinary freedom I give them, they undoubtedly like my style. We're on this journey together, making it up as we go along.

My research is highly anecdotal, but I strongly suspect that your child's active participation in the household could be a leading indicator of their future happiness.

And if you're a kid reading this, you can learn to pitch in and enjoy what the day brings as you lose your fear and resistance to life. You'll become a more valued member of society. You'll have more opportunities for beautiful, stolen moments. You'll have a strategic advantage to ensure your survival.

Helping out with mundane stuff around the house provides an unparalleled opportunity to spend "time with your self" and practice watching feelings arise, dwell and fall away. What am I feeling now? Anger? Gratitude? Joy bubbling up with the dish soap?

Maybe you end up doing the dishes because no matter what you're doing, being alive feels nice. When you're oriented towards the greater good and deepening your experience of aliveness, pleasant experiences do tend to come your way— like your kids admiring your freedom and lightheartedness and wanting to follow along, in the kitchen and out the door. You'll be constantly surprised because each new moment is a divine reflection of what is, and the stream of abundance, the stream of life, just naturally flows your way.

Whether you're a parent or child, as a conscious being, it's your inclination to alleviate suffering wherever and whenever you see it. That pile of dishes in the sink causes your mom to suffer. Save your soul. Roll up your sleeves. And as you become more practiced at being helpful, it may become unclear whether you're pitching in because it makes you feel good or because it makes someone else feel good. Eventually, you'll know it's all the same.

We appreciate that, despite being parent and child, we are all part of a larger genus, the entire family of Beingkind. From algae to elephants, we're all buzzing with Life Stuff— our existence a kind of miracle.

Breathe deep. Remember how good it feels to be you.

You're the writer, director, actor, and audience of your life. And when you're having a moment of identity drama, remember when you were the mountain. Remember when you were the river. Aren't you still? And like water to the dish, remember the ocean of love that surrounds you always.

On Reflection

"Thank God I'm a Country Boy"
~ John Denver

In November of 1999, a few weeks before Thanksgiving, I was scheduled to meet Dr. John Day. He was going to cut out a foot and a half of my lower intestine and the golf ball sized tumor that lived there. I was anxious about the surgery, anxious about dying, and the night before meeting Dr. Day I had another dream.

I was standing on the stage of an old-fashioned movie house and up walked the Dalai Lama. He had a giant smile and gave me a big hug. He said, "It's so good to see you, Richard." And then the dream was over. I woke up feeling better.

I had met His Holiness the Dalai Lama ten years before on a mission to recruit him as a director for The Earth Trust, a non-profit environmental organization that I helped organize with my friends John Haigh and Janette Blainey. I'd sent him a letter describing the new organization and was surprised and delighted that he suggested we come to India to discuss it further. A few weeks later, the three of us spent several private hours with him in his office in Dharamsala. That day he spoke of the laws of interdependence, how everything and everyone is connected, and how important it is to respect the natural environment. He talked of many things that day, though unlike Bill Murray's character in *Caddyshack*, I don't recall His Holiness telling me I'd gain enlightenment in this life. But, I do remember the way his presence filled up the room, which *was* nice (big hitter, The Lama).

He declined to serve as a director, but wrote a very helpful public letter of support for the organization. And though I continued to keep him updated by e-mail for another year or two, I hadn't thought much about him in many years. I wasn't a Buddhist and we sought his involvement in The Earth Trust because of the values that he represented and the good will he engendered.

Still, his presence in my dream left me feeling reassured as I mentally prepared for my visit with Dr. Day, ready to continue my mind-bending, heart-opening path known all too well to those who have heard the words, "You have cancer."

I got myself to the appointment later that morning and was intrigued by all of the nutrition magazines and journals in his waiting room. After all, the guy was a surgeon and not some hocus-pocus energy worker (or so I thought). After exchanging pleasantries, he asked me something I'd felt deeply but was embarrassed to say out loud because it seemed crazy.

"You know this experience is a gift?"

"Yes. I've been feeling exactly that. I don't know if I have a week, a month, or a year to live, but somehow it doesn't matter. I'm learning to feel more deeply, learning to have more compassion for others and myself. Life is more precious now."

"Exactly," he replied.

Dr. Day spoke for an hour that morning and gave me hope that despite the difficulty of my diagnosis, I could heal. Forgetting about the future for a minute, I actually felt better. After the appointment, Alice, who was there with me, said, "Pretty impressive guy...and how about that picture of the Dalai Lama behind his desk?"

"What? I didn't see any picture."

"How could you have missed it?"

"Well, I was just looking at Dr. Day and didn't see the picture." I returned to his office the next day and indeed, there was the picture of His Holiness too big to have been missed. My dream from the night before, and then the picture of His Holiness behind Dr. Day's desk, both deeply reassured me. I was on the right path.

At that time in my life, I had a vague sense of the possibility of seeing Jackson graduate from high school. I could almost feel the future moment as a memory. I also wondered if I was just projecting, maybe looking on from the world of spirit, having already departed. But I had also learned to trust in the power of dreams, the power of feelings, and what I believed to be the non-linear nature of time. It felt reassuring, strange, and as real as can be. I held onto the hope that I would see Jackson graduate from high school and would also be able to see Josh grow up too.

As I write this, Jackson will graduate in exactly one month and Josh is about to finish ninth grade. This past year, I've dialed back my backcountry skiing, been riding my mountain bike a bit more judiciously, living a bit more carefully and cautiously. I don't want to blow it. The last thing I want is to get so close to this moment and then somehow fall victim to my own adrenaline-fueled stupidity. Now, to bear witness to my gratitude and celebration, here is an excerpt from Jackson's graduation party invitation:

> *Soon, when the days are a bit longer, the rain clouds droop a bit closer to this valley, when Dusk infatuates the afternoon with its sharp and sweet glow, as the Earth receives her seeds and the robins arrive in full, I will, amidst all this beauty, be graduating from high school. This passage is to be recognized with a celebration, as warranted by the particular love of this particular's life...Each of you bless me. This is the truth. So thank you with the thanks of each miraculous breath and swoosh of keyboard, with the thanks of wildflowers returning, goats suckling, kiddos warming on hot chocolate or getting a much needed push on the swing, the thanks of receiving clarity, the thanks of real self-acceptance, the thanks of mountain air, the thanks of making art, the thanks of making music, the thanks of mist and sea, of father and mother, fire, water, earth, air, valley, ridge, the thanks of having the opportunity to express gratitude. In the hope that this note finds you in peace, prosperity, and wakeful heartedness . . .*

The boys went to the high school prom last night and Josh was fortunate to have attended as a freshman, invited by a junior girl. This morning, with Josh still asleep, I asked Jackson how the party was. He said it was great. I asked if Josh had a good time and Jackson broke into a big smile, saying, "I don't think anybody had more fun last night than Josh." I took it as testament to my youngest, not quite sixteen and perhaps the most masterful member of our family. He does a great job of managing his reactivity, rarely saying an unkind word or losing his temper, yet he has the capacity to feel deeply, have the most fun at the party. Like everyone, he gets sad or angry too, but he tends not to blame others and is fully capable of self-soothing. And then he reverts to his normal persona, the sensitive-warrior-comedian we all find so adorable. He's pretty inspiring.

Perhaps there will be a follow up to this story when Josh delivers himself to the altar of adulthood in three more years, diploma (and memoir!) in hand.

A few weeks ago, I saw Dr. Day again after twelve years. He had quit his surgery practice a few years back and now is an energy healer and counselor living in Crestone, Colorado. Even though I'm feeling good, I wanted to visit my old friend and see if he had any suggestions to help me feel my best for this transitional moment. And I told him the story of my dream and our first meeting, to which he replied, "You'll be happy to know that the picture of His Holiness you refer to is already on the nightstand in the room you'll be staying.

The Holy Trinity

(the opposite) Sex

When they were 11- and 14-years-old, I asked my boys, "Do you want to be a grocery clerk at sixteen instead of going to college? Have unprotected sex and you might get your wish. Or if you don't hit *that* jackpot, you might get an STD instead. Wait until you are in love to have sex. Use a condom! It's always okay to say no. It's okay to have healthy boundaries. It doesn't matter what anyone thinks of your choices—they just have to feel good to you with the full knowledge and understanding that there are consequences to your actions.

"Having sex, making love, is an intimate act that activates a surge of feelings that the immature person may be ill-equipped to handle. Wild swings of euphoria and depression may result. You may lose your center. A healthy and mature individual doesn't *fall* into love, but rather *ascends* into love. Take time to get to know someone as you take time to know yourself. Let sex be sacred (as opposed to abusive) because as you commune with your beloved, you also commune with God. Merely hooking-up will lead to disappointment and hurt feelings. Your emptiness can't be filled by the next hook-up.

If you didn't get the love you crave from mom or myself, you certainly won't get it from a sexual partner. Wait. Wait. Wait until you're sure."

I also told my boys that, "*All* women are Goddesses. They are special in a way that men can never hope to fully understand. Their body chemistry changes with the moon and the tide. People grow inside of them like aliens. Women deserve special respect and inspire a special sense of wonder and awe. And one day you'll meet a Goddess that craves *your* recognition. By bowing down to her, seeing her in all of her beauty, she'll be able to fully rest in and express her own Divine Femininity. That is a sight to behold."

I also told them of a scene in the movie *As Good As It Gets*, where Jack Nicholson plays a successful author of women's romance novels. He is stopped in an elevator by a gushing fan who asks, "How do you do it? You just seem to get inside of a woman's head." Jack replies, "Well, I just think of a man and then I subtract logic and accountability."

"That," I told my boys, "is what you call a paradox."

As for the actual sex conversation, well, it wasn't really a conversation—it definitely was a lecture, which was out of character for me, but in my mind there was no room for discussion. We were at the dinner table and they just stared at me wide eyed, uncomfortable with the topic and my tone. I left no room for misunderstanding.

The Holy Trinity

Drugs

I began early on the topic of drugs when the boys were around seven and ten. I stuck with the experiential approach and started with a question. Like any good salesman, I knew the answers and wanted them to say yes:

"Can you feel your body growing?"

"Yes."

"I bet that feels good."

"Yes."

"Everyday, cells are growing rapidly, synapses are jumping and hopping in your brain, and if you introduce drugs, alcohol or cigarettes, you may limit the creation of these crucial building blocks for your brain function. You may limit your potential in life. Wait until you're fully-grown, fully developed—maybe in college—before you think about experimenting. There's going to be a lot of pressure to go along with the crowd. I can appreciate your desire to dissociate from disturbing feelings and escape by going numb, but you're taking a big chance with your future. Don't forget who you are. Don't look to others to feel good about yourself. Remember that you can't selectively feel just the fun stuff. Drugs and alcohol can have very severe long term consequences."

I asked them, "Do you think you'll wait to consider if experimenting is right for you and not bow to peer pressure?"

"Yes," they both replied.

This line of reasoning may have been helpful, as both boys have thus far steered clear of drugs and alcohol. And I'm especially grateful to Jackson for having set such a good example for Josh.

To be clear, in no way am I advocating using mind-altering substances at ANY time. I'm just a realist and (so far successfully) hoping to push it off into the distant future. Roseanne Barr once commented that she's done her job as a parent, "if the kids are alive at the end of the day," though perhaps she sets the bar too low.

And as for finding balance as opposed to binging when they get older, I guess I'm just crossing my fingers and hoping for the best. I've offered them wine with dinner since they were ten or twelve and they always say no. Occasionally, if it's something spectacular, I'll insist that they take a tiny sip. And hopefully, with all of the skills they've developed with regard to practicing immediacy, they'll be less drawn to dissociative states, comfortable in managing their own disturbance without needing to go numb, seeing the folly in pretending they're someone else.

[Author's note: I started smoking pot when I was 13. This continued through junior high and high school and my grades suffered accordingly. I wasn't motivated to take the college entrance exams or think of my future. When my friends were heading off to college, I felt pretty stupid.]

Rock n' Roll

You're a kid. Rock out! Don't forget the classics and also explore jazz, folk, hip-hop, bluegrass, classical, and music of other cultures such as African, Celtic, or Brazilian. Whatever you're drawn to is good. Music has an energetic quality that raises your vibration, quiets your mind, and heals your soul. It's the sacred supersonic language of the ancients. Only you know what feels and sounds good to you.

Better yet, *make* music. Play an instrument or just sing as your heart opens inexplicably. Whether you're happy or sad, there's a song for you.

Divorce

After Alice and I separated, I circled back to "we all want to do what's to our benefit," and clearly it was to my benefit to be kind to my ex-wife. Thankfully, she also concluded that it was to her benefit to be kind to me. This didn't mean capitulating to her every whim, but rather keeping a good boundary around what worked for me, expressing myself in a non-reactive and compassionate way. I sought to be an active listener, doing my best to see her perspective too. If both parents (regardless of marriage status) are oriented toward being kind to each other, then there are no major problems, only minor situations.

Alice and I have stayed grounded in this practice and managed to navigate a new friendship that continues to be loving and compassionate, without the bickering that was symptomatic of the final years of our marriage. We're continually learning the same skills we've sought to teach the boys—taking responsibility for our feelings, not blaming the other, using conscious language, and practicing gratitude and service too.

Mind Chatter

It's good to remember that you're not really in charge of your mind and the absurd thoughts and judgments that continually occur to you. You can stand back and witness the steady stream of chatter, and this will prevent you from acting impulsively. Be gentle with yourself as you begin to notice the misconceptions, labels, and violations of others' sovereignty that continually pop into your head. Don't beat yourself up about it. Rather, smile at your folly before you play the fool.

A skillful sovereign treats the egoic mind like an errant child, entertaining to a point, as long as the joke doesn't go too far. Though, ultimately, your ego is an enterprise with no particular value except perhaps to highlight your imagined separation from God. Give your ego a gentle pat on the head and move on. Train yourself to witness your thoughts and catch them before they turn into unskillful words or actions. There's no need to create drama. No need to waste this moment all caught up in your head and unaware of your surroundings.

The mind is generally concerned with telling some story that is set in the past or future, or in some way resisting the present by seeking to label every moment as good or bad. It often tries to distract you from the world of feeling and awareness—of Aliveness Now. In fact, this moment is perfect, though the mind doesn't want you to believe it. It wants you to fear the future by asking you to manipulate, organize, and arrange the next moment instead of allowing it to unfold naturally. Feeling the moment represents death to the ego, and that's why it works so hard to distract you. Alternatively, you can watch your ego from a place of understanding as you rest in your Greater Nature.

When actively observed from a place of neutrality and detached amusement, the ego becomes less and less entertaining with its litany of petty fears and demands. You no longer have a neurotic need to think about what you should do or fear next. You don't have to plot and plan.

And if you're sick of the chatter, you can play a trick and ask yourself, "I wonder what my next thought is going to be?" This exercise stops me in my tracks, always good for a laugh, and invites me to feel alive now.

Notes On Eva and Bruce

Eva Peirrakos was an author that transcribed her "lectures," or teachings that she delivered in a state of deep meditation. She took no credit for the authorship of the material and credited it to a "guide." She lectured extensively on many spiritual topics and over 100 are available free online. Her writings are both precise and poetic and I strongly encourage readers to check this material out.

When I was about 24, Marko had sent me Eva's book *Guide Lectures for Self-Transformation* and, sitting on my girlfriend's sofa in Mill Valley, California on a damp, cool afternoon, I opened it up and began reading.

Several paragraphs into the first lecture entitled "The Call," I experienced an electric current—a full-body energy that was akin to being hit by lightning, but in a good way. Perhaps it's the same current that born-again Christians feel when they're saved, or what Buddhists feel when they experience a moment of enlightenment. Whatever you call it, it leaves you profoundly changed.

Eva says that we are here to gain self-knowledge, self-development, and self-purification for "it is only the purified soul that can stand long in the blinding current of divine love. This is what we fear and yearn for most."

Eva writes about appreciating the difference between egoic consciousness and universal consciousness—the illusion of individuation and separation from God. She suggests that the voice in your head, the ego, rips you away from the truth of the moment. She asks you to notice the resistance to the moment and instead have you connect with what she calls "Universal Consciousness" (or what I refer to as your Greater Nature). She suggests that feeling and life are one and the same.

Eighteen years later, I heard a similar rap in a different wrapper from my teacher Bruce Tift who simply suggested, "Be willing to feel, be aware of your feelings and paradoxically...aware of awareness." Bruce also encouraged me to investigate the "space between my feelings." Perhaps this is what Eva points at too in her lecture titled "Creative Emptiness."

Eva writes that duality is an illusion—there is no "good or bad." Things just are, and identifying with polar opposites makes you unable to experience truth, peace, and love. You raise consciousness among others just by being conscious yourself. You naturally transmute others' unconscious behavior when you don't feel a need to change them, when you don't feel the need to argue. When you operate from the unified plane beyond good and bad, right and wrong, you learn to smile lovingly at misconceptions (including the ones your own ego makes) without anger, malice, or a feeling of self-importance. You welcome the "suchness" that life presents each moment.

Eva would have us believe that our root is pure energy,

consciousness, soul-stuff, ever moving and eternal. As souls we individuated from The Divine so as to play in the cosmos, experience the illusion of separation and the sweetness of union again. Perhaps Buddhists know this experience as the mystical feeling of being One with everything as the lines between self and other blur. You remember your Greater Nature. Bruce simply observes, "We are all one . . . and as we expand our identity to the whole nature of life, embracing the perspective that self is an illusion, we know we can't be threatened. There is nothing that has a separate existence that can be threatened by life."

Every spinning atom is Divine? The essence of each spark no different than that which whirls and twirls in the shape of you? Are there no conventional boundaries to your Greater Nature? My boys seemed to feel it that day at the lake.

That electrified day I was sitting on my girlfriend's sofa in California, that current I felt was unlike anything I'd ever known before. It can only be described as pleasure supreme and there was definitely no thought of "myself" in the picture. For me, it was accompanied by a spontaneous acknowledgment that God is real. That I am beloved. That my soul is eternally connected to the divine. These were the thoughts in my head when I felt this unbelievable surge of energy, lasting for several minutes or more, my entire body buzzing. I've come to believe that the current is always present and it's a matter of choice to plug in at any moment. It seems to be activated when I express gratitude and thanks from deep in my heart. For you atheists out there, I encourage you to investigate this energy source.

Eighteen years later, meeting Bruce for the first time, a few weeks post-op, getting ready to start chemotherapy, I strongly suspected that I might benefit from some counseling. I bounded into his office and he commented on my sprightly comportment. I told him about my situation over the phone prior to our meeting, and I wondered if he noted my energy to make me feel better. Though knowing him now, he undoubtedly gave his observation without an agenda. He was just being present and kind, and already I was feeling better. I sat down and he asked me, "What can I do for you?"

"I'm afraid that I'm going to die," I blurted.

Without missing a beat, Bruce cheerfully replied, "Well, you *are* going to die."

We both just burst out laughing. The truth will indeed set you free.

I came to appreciate one of Bruce's favorite techniques (in addition to his impish grin and razor wit) and often ask myself his question, "What am I avoiding feeling now?" And then, "What's my objection to feeling [the avoided emotion]?" This is effective self-transformation that can be self-administered on the fly. I've learned to give myself permission to feel the truth of my being and believe that beneficial action naturally occurs from this style of inquiry.

Bruce is a Buddhist and (unlike Eva) presumably doesn't believe in God. Though as a Buddhist, he beautifully articulates methods of moving through the world and practical sensibilities that offer unparrallelled potential for self-knowledge, self-development, and self-purification—everything that Eva encourages us to ask of ourselves. Bruce emphasizes Buddhist habits like kindness, compassion, tolerance, open-mindedness, open-heartedness, immediacy, and authenticity.

Eva points to a loving omnipotent, omniscient creative force—God—that permeates all manner of matter and non-matter.

The writer Gustav Flaubert suggested that "God is in the details," while the physicist might wonder if "it's a particle or a wave," and still the Zen Master might observe that "every moment arises, dwells, and falls away."

Maybe what happens is first you hear the call and then look for the details. Or maybe it's the other way around. It's *your Call...*

[Author's note: We recently had live *kirtan* (Indian devotional) music come to our little mountain town and even though I was tired, I dragged myself to the event because I'd been feeling lonely. As the music began, the officiant asked us to set an intention for the evening. I half-heartedly said to myself, "Let the love inside of me come out." Then the music began, and after a few minutes the singer said, "Set your TRUE intention," and I thought to myself, "I wish to meet my beloved." At that moment, I was flooded by that familiar rush of energy and tears began to pour uncontrollably from my eyes as I remembered that my beloved was always inside of me. I said my thanks. Called off the search.

When I later told my friend Carrie Grossman this story, she replied, "Call off the search—I've always loved that sentiment. It's a strange and magical thing, but I've often found that when I call off the search, that which I've been seeking arrives at my door. I continually learn that surrender and receptivity are the best ways to magnetize what I desire, as opposed to aggression and force.]

Cooking

Cooking is a lifelong love of mine. In high school, I was most fortunate to land a job as a cook at a gourmet catering company in Denver, Colorado. To this day, I remember my boss Tom Koehler telling me that cooking is all about timing and sensitivity. Being alert. Understanding the consequences of your actions. Though I didn't realize it at the time, it was my first effort at practicing immediacy—paying very close attention and getting the food just right. Tom also taught me to clean as I went (this tip is worth the price of the book). To wipe up every mess I made and take any free moment to keep my workspace clean. This has been a great lesson for the kids too. It's way more fun to eat a delicious meal if you're not dreading cleaning up the bomb that went off in the kitchen. It's a sign of your developing skill.

Working at Le Petit Gourmet Catering as a kid was the best job in town. A few of the supervisors were graduates of The Culinary Institute of America and by working there I essentially got a paid education. They kept me busy year-round, and with tips I earned $20 or $25 per hour in 1975. As a cook, I learned to be hyper-focused on each moment. How might it look and taste in thirty minutes if you retain the current level of heat? What needs to happen now? Maybe it's nothing. And now. And now. It was a sweet job and

I didn't want to lose it. And as if by magic, thanks to what I'd been taught, I was able to supervise a perfectly prepared prime rib dinner for three hundred people as a 17-year-old slacker.

Being able to prepare great food for friends and family continues to be one of my life's greatest pleasures. Having had that opportunity, I've been delighted to share my enthusiasm with my boys and, like Tom did with me, train them to do things exactly right.

I pat the boys on the back for participation, but I don't sugar coat their performance. There was a time when Jackson was about seven and overcooked the eggs one morning. Rather than praise him for his effort, I was honest. Cheerfully, I questioned, "What the hell is this?" Though he was devastated for an instant, he was able to reflect on having not paid attention and on the resulting brown matter on my plate. He said it "toughened me up, and when praise did come, I took it with all the more satisfaction."

Like my first boss suggested, cooking is made delicious with presence and love. It shines through. And really, I think that this attitude can infuse every activity in your life no matter how mundane. Taking out the trash. Doing the dishes. Tying your shoes. Doing your homework. Writing the report. If you do it with love, you'll like the process and result much better. When you immerse yourself fully in each little step of each action then the sum is much greater than the parts. And you needn't worry about what to do next. Your inner wisdom will guide you. Commit to the process and all sorts of unexpected help will come your way. It may be an idea or an actual helping hand. Or simply knowing when to pull the pie out of the oven at that exact right moment. Do it with presence and love and you'll enjoy the process.

Josh has a natural affinity for the kitchen and he readily grasped the skills required to cook with timing and sensitivity. His offerings are always done with a bit of flair and panache, "Is that white truffle oil on the eggs this morning? Nice!" Josh was making delicious school lunches for himself and his brother every morning from the age of six. Jackson was slower to come around in the kitchen, though he's since made up for lost time, wholly throwing himself into baking bread and creative vegetarian cooking. The kitchen is the hearth, the heart of the home, and as if by magic, as if by alchemy, simple ingredients mixed with love and presence turn into a sacred and nourishing celebration.

Recipes

Brian's Potato Salad

. . . is THE bomb and is the cornerstone of the best picnic lunch ever. It's not even debatable.

New potatoes, roasted red peppers (bottled or fresh), hard-boiled egg (quartered), celery (chopped), moroccan or black olives (pitted), red onion (chopped), lots of parsley (chopped). Cook the potatoes the night before and then refrigerate, or if it's the same day, at least give them time to cool. Then chop the potatoes into pieces ¾ of the size of your thumb. Make a dressing from mayo, olive oil, cajun spices from a mix or just use paprika and cayenne. Using a large bowl, mix all of the ingredients together and then pour the dressing on top, going easy on the dressing. Add the hard-boiled eggs last as they will break down with too much tossing. Add salt and pepper. Serve with bbq chicken and watermelon.

Asparagus Vinaigrette

One bunch of asparagus, organic if possible. If the ends are brownish, cut them off but you should be able to use most of the stalk. Chop three or four big cloves of garlic, again, organic if possible. Put the asparagus into a pan of boiling water for no more than two minutes. They need to stay crunchy! Remove and drain through a colander. Place the warm and dry asparagus on a plate and drizzle with olive oil (the fancier the better), syrupy balsamic vinegar (Villa Manodori from Williams Sonoma is my fave), and then toss the chopped garlic on. Add fresh cracked pepper and fancy salt (Ile de Re' - also available from Williams Sonoma). Allow the asparagus to sit at room temp for an hour and then it's game on.

Brussel Sprouts

Cut the sprouts in half lengthwise and place with the skin down in a Pyrex dish. Drizzle olive oil over them and place in the oven at 375 until they just begin to brown. It should be in the neighborhood of 35 minutes. Chop several cloves of garlic and remove the almost brown sprouts from the oven. Spread the chopped garlic on the sprouts and drizzle a bit more olive oil on them. Return to the oven until they almost fully brown and then turn off the heat, leaving them in the oven to slowly finish and stay warm. Chop a tart green apple into paper thin slices, crush a handful of pistachio nuts and make a sauce of sour cream and melted butter, adding a dash of water to the mixture if you'd like. Remove the brussels sprouts from the oven, generously salt them and place on a warm plate. Top with the apple slices, crushed pistachios (or hazelnuts), and drizzle over the *creme fraiche* sauce you made. If you'd like, this can all be served over fresh greens as a warm winter salad, and you can substitute fancy, syrupy balsamic vinegar for the *creme fraiche* sauce, but you may want to leave out the apples and nuts. Try a bit of kiwi or sliced red grapes instead. THIS recipe is worth the price of the book. No doubt.

Josh's Vegitarian Panini

Slice your favorite locally made bread. Cover both slices with dijon mustard, then drizzle with honey. Saute up your favorite veggies. Josh likes to use onion, peppers, chard, garlic, and mushroom. Just before the saute is done, add fresh arugula or spinach. Slice your favorite cheese. Hint: the veggies go well with swiss or goat cheese. Put the veggie mix from the sauté pan on the sliced bread and then top with cheese. Add a slice of tomato (optional). Close up sandwich and place a bit of butter on the panini maker or in a pan if you're using the stovetop. Stovetop directions: Press down firmly with a spatula and flip when bread begins to brown. Serve with pickle (and chips!). And a lemonade would be nice.

Chicken in a Skillet

Place a whole chicken upside down in a skillet. Add a cup each of chopped carrot, potato and onions and spread around the perimeter of the bird. Place in the oven at 350 for about 45 minutes or until the bottom begins to brown just a bit. Pull the pan out of the oven and flip the bird and maybe give the veggies a stir too. After another hour in the oven or until it is not quite brown (it depends on the size of the bird), pull the pan out and remove the whole chicken, placing it on a cutting board. Remove the thighs, legs, and breasts and place back in the skillet. Turn on the broiler for five or ten minutes until the bird browns and be careful to not overcook. Oh, and there will be plenty of juices in the pan which could be spooned over the veggies and chicken before returning to the oven to brown.

Serve buffet style right out of the pan with generous

amounts of fresh chopped parsley and a bit of salt and pepper. It's an entire meal in a pan and it's making me hungry just thinking about it.

Leek Fritters and Arugula salad

Cut 3 leeks into 1 in. thick slices. Saute them in olive oil along with a handful of finely cut shallots until they are soft. Then place them in a large bowl, and add a touch of cayenne pepper, 1/2 cup of chopped parsley, 1 tsp. of coriander, 1 tsp. of cumin, 1/2 tsp. of turmeric, 1/4 tsp. of cinnamon, and 1/2 tsp. of salt. Let it cool. Whisk an egg white and fold it into the leeks. In a separate bowl mix 1 egg, 2/3 cup milk, 4 1/2 tsp of melted butter, 3/4 cup flour, and 1 tbsp of baking powder. Mix it into the liquidy leeks. Fry the battered leeks as you would pancakes. Serve on a bed of arugula, squeeze a bit of lemon and salt to taste.

The Best Chocolate Chip Cookies Ever

2 1/4 cups all-purpose flour 1 teaspoon baking powder 1 teaspoon salt . 1 cup (two sticks) butter softened 3/4 cup granulated sugar 3/4 cup firmly packed light brown sugar 1 teaspoon vanilla 24 ounces chocolate chips 1 cup nuts. Preheat oven to 375°F. In small bowl combine flour, baking powder and salt , set aside. In large bowl add cream butter, sugars and vanilla until smooth and fluffy beat in one egg at a time blend in flour mixture, chocolate chips and drop by rounded spoonfuls onto on greased baking sheet bake 8 to 10 minutes until golden. Double the recipe. They will disappear.

Breakfast Suggestions and Egg Methodology

Cooking eggs (or anything) is all about timing and sensitivity. First, you put the butter in the pan and allow it to get hot, but not burn. I use the medium-high setting. Then you put the toast in the toaster. Then you crack the egg gently and lightly stir the runny white part of the egg without touching the yolk. Within a minute or two the egg is almost ready. Gently flip the egg with a rubber spatula and then turn the heat off. The egg will continue to slowly finish and allow you a nice margin for error to get your plate ready. The eggs stay hot, but don't overcook.

Our house is often a bit chilly, so I'll take the plates and hold them over the flame on the stove to take the chill off of them. Putting hot food on a cold plate is a rookie error. The food gets cold before it's even served!

So, by this time the toast is done, then gets buttered, and the egg that's hot but not overcooked are all placed on the warm plate. But before this entire procedure takes place, perhaps a few strawberries or a grapefruit was sliced to place on the dish too. You don't want to be scurrying around to finish while the cooked food is getting cold. Like magic, it all comes together perfectly with a bit of presence and forethought. If you teach timing and sensitivity from the start, kids can learn to cook eggs (and other dishes) exactly the way you like them.

Jackson is more likely to serve baked eggs with arugula, goat's yogurt, and lots of fresh garlic. A stinky and delicious favorite of ours. And he might serve it all up with a smoothie made of cucumber, apple, ginger, and lime. That is if we're lucky. Sometimes he'll throw a bunch of chard, spinach, spirulina, and maybe an apple for good luck into the blender, which is undoubtedly healthy, and also disturbingly dank. Which rhymes with rank. Hold your nose and gulp is my strategy, though admittedly I have developed an affinity, or at least a tolerance, for these super-green drinks in the morning.

I have also become something of a zealot in my pursuit of zero food waste. Put that rubbery celery in the blender with some water and a scoop of spirulina powder. Disgusting, I know. Better to rotate the food in the fridge so nothing gets lost, avoiding these unpleasant culinary experiments.

Meat Methodology

The trick to cooking steaks or burgers is to sear it then put it in the oven to finish. Place a cast iron skillet on the stove at a high heat. Use a bit of olive oil in the pan. Toss the meat in and allow it to sizzle. Get brown on one side. Then flip it over and immediately put it in the oven at 300. It will continue searing on the other side. Pull it out of the oven and flip every few minutes if its a steak. A burger can just finish without disturbance, depending on its thickness. By searing the steak you seal in the juices and by finishing cooking at a low temp it takes longer but you have a much bigger margin for error. If unsure, cut into a tiny corner to check as you flip. When 90% done, pull it out of the oven, cover and rest as you finish the plates, warm the buns, whatever. Perfect burgers and steaks every time.

Spicy Fruit Salsa

I use organic kiwis, raspberries, mango, and seedless grapes. Chop and toss them in a spicy honey marinade, made from fresh lime juice, puréed habanero peppers, chopped Spanish onion, chopped red and green pepper, and plenty of cilantro. Let this all marinate for 15 minutes. This salsa is best served the day it is made and if your fruit is really sweet, you may want to cut back on the honey.

Spinach Pie

This recipe requires five pounds of fresh spinach, organic if possible. Picked, washed and torn into pieces. Add olive oil to sauté pan with a small amount of garlic and onion, quickly cook spinach until bright green. It will take sautéing in several batches. Squeeze all excess liquid out of the cooked spinach, put aside to cool. Next layer FILO dough in sheet pan and brush with ghee. Add more FILO until you have 7-10 sheets on the bottom. Always brush sheets with ghee in between. Add spinach and repeat layering until all of the spinach is gone. Use only 3-4 sheets of FILO in middle of the pie. I sometimes add feta to the mix somewhere in the middle of the pie. Season the top liberally with salt and pepper, bake at 400 for 20 minutes. Let cool completely before cutting. Best served grilled and lightly warm.

Robin's Chicken Soup in a Crock Pot

Take a whole chicken, wash and pat dry, put in crock pot with onion, carrot, celery and black peppercorns and enough water to cover. Set on low setting and let cook at least 24

hours. Remove bird from broth and let cool. Mash remaining veggies in pot and continue cooking.Sautée onions, carrots, celery and garlic in butter. Add to broth and
continue cooking meanwhile seperate chicken from the
bones. Add to the pot and continue cooking for 4 hours on
low. Season with salt and pepper and fresh herbs. I like to use
parsley, chives, oregano and thyme.

Have this soup on hand in the freezer. It tends to sooth a
cold and make you feel better, nourished.

Laura's Mountain Earth Muffins

Don't miss Thursdays at Mountain Earth Health Foods in
Crested Butte as Laura makes the best muffins you've ever
tasted. For real. Or if you're not in the neighborhood, now
you can make them at home.

Sunrise Muffins (Vegan)
This recipe makes 2 servings (12 large muffins):

2 cups spelt flour
2 cups whole spelt flour
1 cup oats
1 cup flaxseed meal
2 tsp baking soday
1 tsp sea salt
3 Tbsp Cinnamon
3 Tbsp Cardamom
1 1/3 cup coconut milk (or any non-dairy milk)
1 1/3 cup maple syrup
1 cup of coconut oil
2 apples (1 cup) - diced finely

1/2 to 1 cup carrots - shredded
1/2 cup of pumpkin or sunflower seeds
1 cup of nuts
1 cup of dried fruit

Bake for 30-40 minutes at 350 degrees. You can tell when there done by inserting a toothpick - if it comes out clean they are good to go!

Notes: you can do a lot of variations with this recipe. I tend to do an apricot almond one, Where I use a cup of dried apricots (or fresh if you have them) and a cup of almonds. I also do a ginger pecan with a cup of candied ginger and a cup of pecans.

The prep is pretty simple, just mix it all together, spray the muffin cups with coconut oil (or whatever you've got) and scoop it in. You can fill the muffin cups pretty high because they don't rise too much. Also, to cut the carrots and apples I use a food processor so it all blends in well together.

Acknowledgements

For love, feedback and encouragement thanks to:

Jackson, Josh, Robin, Alissa Johnson (my brilliant editor), Kia Portafekas, Ben Ewing, Zoya Bahn, Jordan O'Neil, Arvin Ram, Arthur Kaufman, Carrie Grossman, Mark Reaman, Carrie Jo Chernoff, Carla Zizo, Caleb Seeling, Darin Portnoy, Dave Penney, Corina and Amos Dunlap, Tom Laughlin, Brian Halloran, Bruce Tift, John Day, Todd Wasinger, Paula Martone, Wendy Fisher, Jenny McGruther, Hillary Maley, Lee Ann Canty, Stephanie Phillips, Ivan Ussach, Laurie Sude, Juliette Eymere, Ginny and Geo Bullock, Sue Sherman, David Rothman and Kate Seeley.

And thanks to my own folks for hosting me, Larry Melnick and Joanie Talpers.